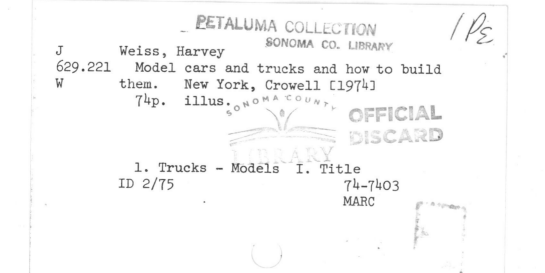

MODEL CARS AND TRUCKS

AND HOW TO BUILD THEM

BY HARVEY WEISS

THE GADGET BOOK

HOW TO MAKE YOUR OWN BOOKS

MODEL CARS AND TRUCKS
   AND HOW TO BUILD THEM

MOTORS AND ENGINES
   AND HOW THEY WORK

SHIP MODELS
   AND HOW TO BUILD THEM

MODEL CARS AND TRUCKS

AND HOW TO BUILD THEM

by Harvey Weiss

illustrated with
photographs, plans,
and drawings

THOMAS Y. CROWELL COMPANY
NEW YORK

All the models illustrated were made by the author
with the exception of the two on page 72. The upper
one was built by John Weiss, the lower one by Mat-
thew Morris. Photographs are by the author.

LIBRARY OF CONGRESS CATALOGING IN PUBLICATION DATA
Weiss, Harvey.
Model cars and trucks and how to build them.
SUMMARY: Introduces the tools, materials, and techniques for
creating a variety of model cars and trucks.   1. Automo-
biles—Models—Juv. lit.   2. Motortrucks—Models—Juv. lit.
[1. Trucks—Models]   I. Title.   TL237.W44   629.22'1
74-7403   ISBN 0-690-00414-1

10   9   8   7   6   5   4   3

CONTENTS

INTRODUCTION

Most of the cars and trucks in this book can be built so that they are fairly accurate copies of the real thing. The racing car shown here, for example, is a copy of the sort of modern car used on international racing circuits. It is quite realistic, and it could be even more accurate if more details were added.

But the cars and trucks described in this book are really most enjoyable in their own right—not because they look exactly like an actual car or truck. They are models of something, to be sure. They are based on real cars and trucks. But they are fun *in themselves* and not because they are a substitute for or imitation of the real thing.

Making a model car is a little like painting a landscape. The painter does not try to make a precise copy of what he sees. He uses the scene as the basis for a painting which is pleasing in itself. When someone else looks at the finished painting, he either likes it or not because of the colors and the composition, not because it is an accurate or inaccurate copy of the original scene.

This is the way I feel about the models in this book. I find them interesting and pleasing by themselves, and I don't really care if they are very accurate or not. They are fun to make. They are fun to have around. If they have the general feeling and mood of the car or truck they are based on, that is enough and I am perfectly satisfied.

These model cars and trucks can be displayed on a desk, in a bookcase, or on a shelf. I find that my models end up on window sills, the kitchen counter, the coffee table in the living room—in fact, they look fine anywhere at all. There is one car, however, that is a little too large to go on a shelf. That is the coaster—described in chapter 10—which you can actually ride on.

The directions on the following pages tell you how to put together the models illustrated in the photographs. But there is absolutely no reason why you have to make these models just as they are shown. You can modify them any way you want, making whatever changes and improvements you feel like making. The directions are quite exact about technical matters—how to make a fender, attach an axle, and so on. But sizes, shapes, placement of parts, styling, color, are all up to you. You can design your own car or truck according to your own ideas.

Don't be alarmed if some of the models illustrated look slick and difficult to make. They aren't! They are planned so that they can be built with no expert skills. The trick is that when you start to make one of these cars or trucks, you must think of one thing at a time. The truck shown opposite, for example, may seem fairly complicated. But it is no more than a combination of twenty-one little pieces of wood—all of them (not counting the wheels) simple square or rectangular shapes. If you can cut out a small, neat square of wood, you can make this truck. The other model—the shiny convertible—is also a quite simple job of carpentry. The car looks so sleek and elegant only because

2

a great deal of time and care were taken to get a well-sand-papered, perfectly smooth, carefully painted surface.

But there is one thing you do need, and it is important. That is the patience to work slowly and carefully. Don't be in a hurry! If you rush you will get a sloppy job.

1. THE TOOLS AND MATERIALS

THE TOOLS

Very few people have all the tools listed here. If you find that you don't have exactly the right tool for the job, see if you can't figure out some other way of doing it. Or else change the design of your car or truck so that it can be built with the tools you do have.

Many people have tools that have been lying about in an old box or kitchen drawer and have become dull and rusty. You can clean and sharpen some tools, such as screwdrivers or chisels, but dull hacksaw blades, or files, or small, cheap saws, can't be fixed. Throw them out and get new ones. There is nothing as annoying and pointless as trying to shape wood with a dull file, or trying to cut a board with a dull saw. A few dollars spent on new, good-quality tools is always a good investment.

SAWS The most important kind of saw for model making is a coping saw, shown here. It has a thin blade so that it can cut all kinds of curves and small details. The blade can be turned in its frame to face in any direction you want. Large carpenter's saws are good for cutting up planks or roughing out shapes. A hacksaw is used primarily for cutting metal, but can also be used to cut wood.

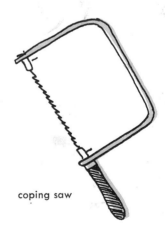

coping saw

RASPS AND FILES These are useful for smoothing out rough shapes. A rasp is coarser than a file. A good rasp with big, coarse teeth will remove an amazing amount of wood in short order.

SHAPER This is a recently developed tool that is a little like a file. The difference is that it has a replaceable blade with openings behind the cutting teeth. Wood shavings can escape through these openings, so the blade never clogs up. When it gets dull the blade can be simply replaced. The shaper, like any cutting tool, must be used either with the grain of the wood or across the grain— never against the grain. If you cut against, your cutting tool will snag and splinter the wood.

HAND DRILL To drill holes, you will need this tool as well as a variety of different-size bits. Useful bit sizes are $\frac{1}{16}$ inch, $\frac{1}{8}$ inch, $\frac{3}{16}$ inch, $\frac{1}{4}$ inch, $\frac{3}{8}$ inch. (You can use a nail in your drill if you cut off the head. This works fine for making smaller-size holes.)

SQUARE Whenever you want to make a right angle cut across a piece of wood, you need a square. This will let you pencil a line that goes squarely across the wood. Follow this line with your saw and you have a true cut. If you don't have a square you can substitute the sort of plastic triangle used in mechanical drawing, or anything that you know is square. Use a book if nothing else is available.

HAMMER AND NAILS There are times when you will want a hammer and nails. Thin nails with small heads, called "brads," are most useful. Be careful to use the right size of nail. Too big a nail will split a small piece of wood. Too thin or too short a nail won't hold well. If you suspect that a nail may split the wood, drill a hole first where the nail is to go. The hole should be slightly smaller than the diameter of the nail.

GLUE The models in this book have all been assembled with Elmer's glue. This is very strong and quick-drying. If you don't have this kind of glue, any similar white glue will do—or for that matter any fast-drying glue intended for use with wood will work well. Paper paste or rubber cement won't hold and should never be used. Remember that the surfaces to be joined must be smooth and even. Don't try to glue surfaces which are rough or bumpy—they won't stick together with any strength or permanence.

Most glues intended for use with wood will work best if some pressure is used to hold the wooden parts together. This can be done with clamps or by putting a weight on top of the glued parts. With a white glue like Elmer's, a half hour of pressure is recommended. However, I've found that if the surfaces to be joined are straight and even and if the glue is applied liberally, I can hold the parts together with my fingers for three or four minutes and the joint will be strong and permanent.

SANDPAPER All models have to be very carefully and thoroughly sanded if they are to look nice. (It is usually much easier to sandpaper small parts *before* they are glued in place.) You'll need rough, medium, and fine sandpaper. Sandpaper is described by grit number: 40- or 60-grit is rough, 80-grit is medium, 150- and up is fine. Look for these numbers printed on the back of the sheet. Get the

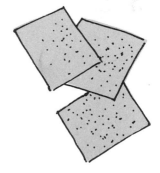

better quality of sandpaper, which is called "production grade." It will last much longer than the cheaper variety.

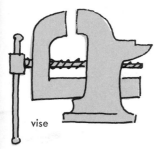
vise

VISE A holding device of some kind is a very important tool. A vise—the bigger the better—will do the job best. But if you don't have one, a large C-clamp can be used to hold your wood to the worktable while you saw or file. When you put a piece of woodwork in a vise, use two scraps of wood to protect the surfaces. Otherwise the metal jaws will leave scars. You could also protect the work by wrapping the jaws of the vise with tape.

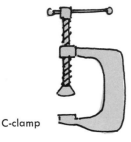
C-clamp

These are the essential tools, but there are any number of other useful ones that you may have available. You will certainly have a screwdriver and pocketknife. You may also find some chisels, which can come in handy. However, any cutting tools such as knives or chisels are worse than useless unless they are really sharp. So if you want to use these tools you must also have a sharpening stone.

Another useful tool that many people have is an electric drill. If this is fitted with a coarse-sanding disk, the finishing of your models can be greatly speeded up.

THE MATERIALS

The models described on these pages use very ordinary lumber, of the sort you may find lying about the house or in any lumber yard. The most common sizes needed are boards measuring 1×2 inches and $\frac{1}{2} \times 2$ inches. Wood of $\frac{1}{4}$- or $\frac{3}{8}$-inch thickness is also used a great deal. This thin wood (not plywood) is available from the lumber yard in

various widths up to 3½ inches and in lengths up to 8 feet or more. Sometimes it is called "lattice" wood, sometimes "stripping," sometimes "molding." But if you simply ask for a piece of pine wood ¼ inch thick, 3 inches wide, and 6 feet long (for example), you'll get the right thing.

It is worth remembering that the sizes of lumber given refer to the *unfinished* size of the piece. The actual wood you get won't necessarily measure the size mentioned. For example, a piece of "1 × 2" may actually measure ¾ × 1¾ inches. The reason for this is that the wood you get has been planed down by the sawmill. You get a smooth board, but it is smaller than when it started.

It is generally best to avoid plywood. This is strong wood useful for many purposes, but it isn't very good for model making. It is difficult to cut without getting splintered edges, and it often has an overly noticeable grain pattern. In general, it ends up looking a lot less neat than you would like.

Balsa wood is a very light, porous material that is sometimes used in model making, particularly airplane models.

It could be used to make the models described in this book, but you will be much better off with regular lumber. Models made of balsa wood will turn out to be rather delicate and weak.

You probably won't always have the size of lumber you need. This is no reason for concern because it is a very simple matter to glue together several smaller pieces to get what you want. If, on the other hand, the wood you have is too wide or too large, it can be cut down to size. Actually almost any of the trucks and cars in this book can be built with a length of 1 × 2-inch board, a dowel, and a few feet of thin wood.

The best kind of wood for our purposes is clear pine. This has no knotholes and is easily cut and sanded. There are other kinds of lumber, of course, and they all can be used. Mahogany, cedar, apple, redwood, and many other sorts of wood are fine for model making. In fact some of these woods have such nice color and grain patterns that you may want to leave the finished model unpainted. Very hard woods, such as maple, are best avoided.

If you are using miscellaneous old junk-pile lumber, choose the sections that are free of knotholes, splits, and warps. Don't worry about nail holes—these can be easily patched. And don't be put off if the wood you find is discolored or painted. A file or sandpaper will get you down to a fresh surface in a few minutes, and the wood may turn out to be just what you wanted.

Another form of wood that is much used in model making is dowels. These are wooden rods which come in many different diameters, from 1 inch down to ⅛ inch. They are sold in 3-foot lengths. Dowels are useful for axles and ladders, and in general are good things to have around.

2. FINISHING AND PAINTING

The way a model car or truck is finished has a great deal to do with the way it finally looks. Sloppy paint with drips and sags, or rough spots that could have been sanded away will spoil what might otherwise be a very nice-looking model. Here is the right way to do it.

First, do any necessary patching. Cracks, gouges, holes, can be filled with a commercial patching material such as Plastic Wood. If you don't have any of this, you can make your own patching mixture by combining glue with the fine dust you get when you file or sandpaper wood. Give the patch plenty of time to dry before sanding it down.

Sand everything very carefully, using a block of wood to wrap your sandpaper around. This "backup" block for your sandpaper is important. It keeps the sandpaper bearing down evenly on the surface you are smoothing. If you hold the sandpaper in your hand without the block, the bumps on the surface you are finishing will stay high and the valleys will stay low. What you'll end up with is smooth bumps and valleys, not a straight, level surface. When you are sanding small parts, simply lay the paper down on a flat surface and rub the part back and forth on the paper. Sandpaper will last longer if you fold it as

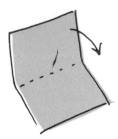

1. Fold in half.

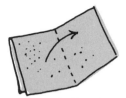

2. Fold in half again.

3. Cut along one of the folds.

The paper will look like this when it is unfolded. Now you can fold it up again, but do so in such a way that no two rough surfaces are rubbing against one another.

shown in the drawing in the margin. This way you never have one sandpaper surface rubbing against another, wearing itself out to no purpose.

If separate parts of your model are to be painted different colors, do the painting *before* you assemble the parts. When two painted parts are to be glued together, leave unpainted the area where the parts will touch. You can use a bit of tape to keep the paint off such an area. If you were to glue a painted surface to another painted surface, you would actually be gluing a layer of paint to another layer of paint—not wood to wood. The paint is liable to peel off the wood, and your model would come apart.

When the sanding is done (make sure you do a good job), dust off the surface thoroughly and paint on a sealer coat such as shellac or varnish. This seals the grain of the wood. Let it dry, then sand with fine sandpaper. Dust off again. (If you don't have any shellac or varnish you can skip this step, in which case you will probably have to put on a few extra coats of paint.)

Now you can begin to paint. If possible, get a can of aerosol spray paint. This will produce a perfect finish if you follow the directions on the label. The idea with this kind of paint is to use many very thin coats. Sand and dust after the first two or three coats. Allow plenty of time for each coat to dry—and don't despair if the paint job looks terrible at the start. Eight or ten coats may be necessary for a really nice finish.

If you don't have any spray paint, use whatever house or furniture paint you do have. This may require two or more coats. Use a good wide, soft brush—an old, stiff-whiskered brush won't put down a smooth, even layer of paint. Sand with fine sandpaper after the first coat. Be sure one coat is dry before you put on the next. Most cars look best with a glossy enamel finish, but this is a matter for you to decide.

When you are painting on small details, like radiators or hub caps or numbers, use a fine, pointed brush such as a watercolor brush. And of course all brushes should be carefully cleaned after use. An oil-base paint is cleaned off with turpentine, and a water-base paint with water. Do a good job or the brush won't perform well for you the next time you need it.

If you have used nice wood for your model and like the way it looks, and if there isn't too much patching, you may decide you don't want to paint at all. In this case it isn't a bad idea to brush on some shellac or varnish, or rub in some floor wax. This will help to keep the wood from getting soiled and finger-marked.

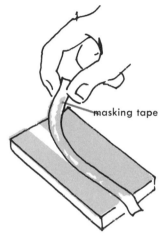

masking tape

When an area or a part of a model is to be painted in more than one color, follow this procedure: 1. Paint the entire area in one color. 2. When the paint is dry, press down masking tape along the line where the second color is to begin. 3. Paint on the second color, going slightly over the edge of the masking tape. Don't use too much paint at the edge, and brush the paint away from the tape so that it won't crawl up under the tape. 4. Peel off the tape, and you'll find a clean, sharp, straight edge where the two colors meet. This procedure can also be used for painting stripes. In this case you would use two pieces of masking tape and paint your second color between them.

3. HOW TO MAKE THE WHEELS

The most important part of any car or truck is the wheels. You may build a beautiful body and give the model a magnificent paint job—but if the wheels aren't round, or if they wobble, the final result will be disappointing. Wheels are important, and they are also tricky to make right. So this chapter is devoted only to wheels, and to the different ways of making and attaching them.

If you happen to know somebody who has some power woodworking tools, you may be able to persuade him to make some wheels for you. This is the easy way out. Wheels can be easily turned on a lathe, or cut out of a plank of wood by means of a hole cutter attached to a drill press or electric hand drill. They can also be cut out with a band saw or electric jigsaw.

But if none of this equipment is available, you will have to use one of the methods described here. The simplest method is just to cut out the wheels from a board using a coping saw. Most of the wheels used in the models in this book have been cut out of ½-inch-thick board. In certain cases, however, such as the back wheels of some racing cars, you might want to use a thicker board to get a heavier wheel. And in the case of antique cars you might want to use a thinner board to get a more delicate-looking wheel. This is how to cut them out.

thumbtack

hole in cardboard

cardboard

If you round off the edges of the
wheel, it will look more realistic.

1. Use compasses to draw the outline of the wheel. If you don't have compasses, punch a hole in a piece of cardboard and use it as shown.

2. After the circle is drawn on the board, punch a dent with a nail at the center point. Then drill a hole. If the wheel is going to be attached to a dowel axle, the hole should be of a size that the dowel will fit into exactly. If the wheel is going to be held in place by a wood screw, the hole size should be right for the screw you are planning to use. It is best to drill the hole *before* cutting out the wheel because sometimes the drill will wander slightly off center as you use it. If this were to happen after the wheel was cut out, you would have to throw it away. It is important that you drill a straight hole—it should be exactly at right angles to the wood. If it is not true, the wheel will wobble. Take your time and be careful.

3. Put your board in a vise if you have one, or clamp it to your worktable, and cut along the outside edge of the compass line. Be sure to keep the saw perpendicular to the wood.

4. After the wheel is cut out, go over it with a file and then sandpaper to remove any bumps or rough spots. Make sure it is perfectly round.

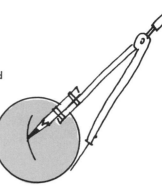

If you have a blank wheel and want to find the center point, use this method. With compasses draw a small arc. The point of the compasses should touch the edge of the wheel. The distance from the point of the compasses to the pencil point should be slightly more than the radius of the wheel.

Do this three times, with the point of the compasses at three different places along the edge of the wheel.

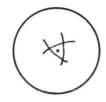

A spot in the center of the three arcs will be the center of the circle.

Another way to make a wheel is from a pole of some sort. In this case all you have to do is slice off whatever thickness you need, then drill a hole for the axle. An old rolling pin will provide quite a few large wheels. A broomstick handle or wooden curtain rod can also be used. Of course these will make wheels of rather small diameter.

If you make a wheel from a pole or thick rod of some sort, you are going to be faced with the problem of finding the exact center of the circle. Rather than making a guess, use the method shown here.

Another possible source of wheels is the ends of thread spools. Most of them are a little too small for our purposes. But you may be lucky and find some fairly big spools, and in that case you can cut off the ends and have some fine wheels. Two or three poker chips cemented together will make an excellent wheel, and an old checker set or backgammon set presents still other possibilities.

Still another source of wheels is old, broken toys. Many of the wheels you'll find this way are flimsy, unpleasant plastic objects. But you may be able to discover some that are well made and of the right size. If you do find a set of suitable wheels from an old toy, you will have to figure out how to remove them. Sometimes a determined twist will pull them loose. In other cases you can cut away the parts of the old toy that are holding them in place. Occasionally you will have to use a hacksaw and cut the axle

17

apart. You will also have to find a way of attaching the wheels to your model. In most cases a sturdy nail or screw will hold this kind of wheel in place.

TIRES

Most of the models shown in this book don't have any tires. If a wooden wheel is painted black around the edges, the general impression of a tire is given. However, it is not difficult to make a wheel with an actual rubber tire. The trick is to find a piece of suitable rubber hose. This can be cut into narrow slices to be fitted over the wooden wheels. You can make the wheel of a size that will suit the tire.

A conventional garden hose is a little too small for most car model wheels. But you may be able to find an old hose from an automobile radiator, or the kind of hose that is used for the drain of a washing machine. A bicycle inner tube is a bit too thin to make a very convincing-looking tire, but you can double them up—one on top of another.

You can also make a tire out of a flat sheet or strip of rubber. The kind of rubber used for bathtub mats or automobile floormats will make fine tires. You will have to cut the rubber into strips as wide as the edges of the wheels. Then cut to length and glue in place with contact cement, epoxy cement, or rubber cement.

ATTACHING THE WHEELS

The simplest way of attaching a wheel to the body of a car or truck is with a long wood screw. If the screw is long enough and sturdy enough and is screwed into a solid

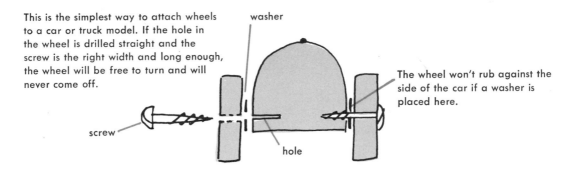

This is the simplest way to attach wheels to a car or truck model. If the hole in the wheel is drilled straight and the screw is the right width and long enough, the wheel will be free to turn and will never come off.

washer

The wheel won't rub against the side of the car if a washer is placed here.

screw

hole

piece of wood, the wheel is never going to come off. When you attach a wheel this way, be sure to drill a hole for the screw first. The hole should be just slightly smaller than the diameter of the screw. It is also important that you make all four screw holes at the same distance up from the bottom of the car or truck body. If you do this, you can be certain that all four wheels will rest on the ground. A jiggly car that rides on only three wheels at a time can be rather annoying.

Wood screws are used to attach the wheels of this racing car. In cars of this type the rear wheels are usually wider than the front ones and therefore require slightly longer screws.

In many of the models described in this book the wheels are permanently attached to the axle, which is a wooden dowel. Both wheels and the axle turn together. This is a sturdy arrangement—the wheels aren't liable to wobble or come loose. If you have a ¼-inch dowel, drill a ¼-inch hole in your wheels and you can be sure the dowel will fit snugly. Usually it is such a tight fit that you don't even need glue to hold the wheels in place.

There are a number of different ways of attaching axles to a model car or truck. Some of the possibilities are shown here. The method you choose will depend on the kind of model you are making and also on what materials you have to work with.

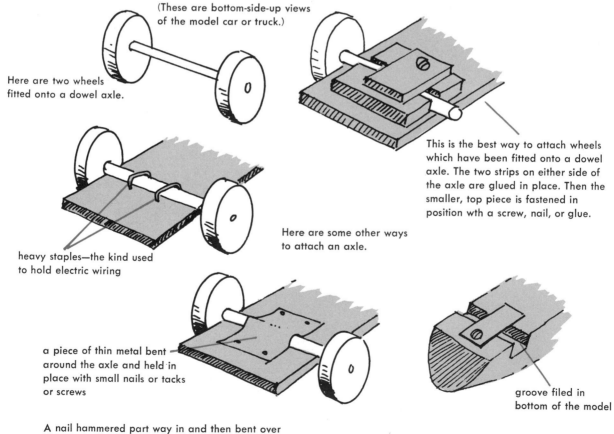

(These are bottom-side-up views of the model car or truck.)

Here are two wheels fitted onto a dowel axle.

This is the best way to attach wheels which have been fitted onto a dowel axle. The two strips on either side of the axle are glued in place. Then the smaller, top piece is fastened in position wth a screw, nail, or glue.

heavy staples—the kind used to hold electric wiring

Here are some other ways to attach an axle.

a piece of thin metal bent around the axle and held in place with small nails or tacks or screws

groove filed in bottom of the model

A nail hammered part way in and then bent over will sometimes hold an axle securely, but looks rather sloppy.

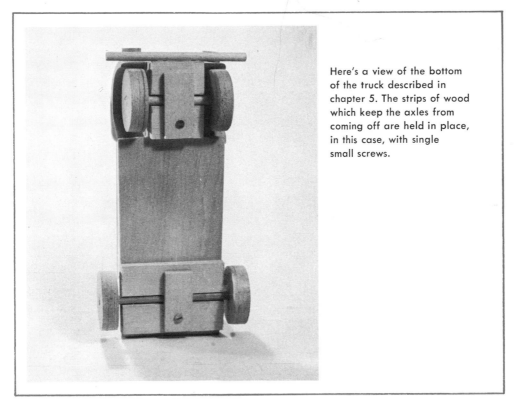

Here's a view of the bottom of the truck described in chapter 5. The strips of wood which keep the axles from coming off are held in place, in this case, with single small screws.

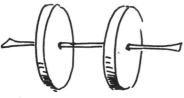

If you are using metal or plastic wheels from an old toy or model you may need an axle. Sometimes a piece of coat hanger wire with the ends hammered flat will hold the wheels quite securely. Put the wheels on the axle—then hammer the ends flat. In some cases a nail or thin screw will hold the wheels in place.

There may be times when you want to attach wheels to a thin strip of wood. If the wood is too thin a screw might split it. In a case such as this it is best to glue on a small block of wood and then screw the wheel onto that.

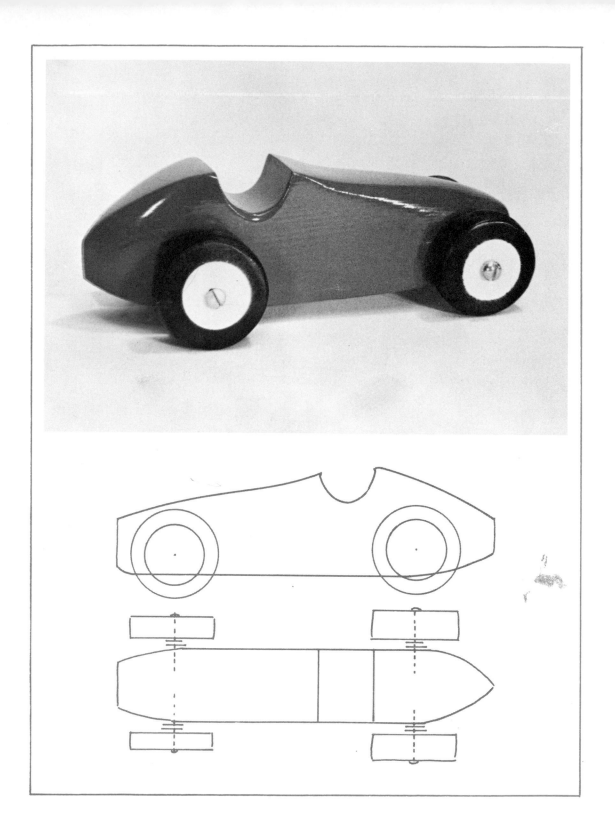

4. RACING CARS

These racing cars are quite simple to make. Aside from the wheels there is only one piece of wood.

The car illustrated here is based more or less on the racers that competed on the international circuits of the 1920s and 1930s. They were relatively small and stubby cars, with speeds which rarely exceeded 100 miles an hour. But they were elegant-looking machines, in bright colors and with graceful shapes. Cars of this type bore the exotic names still familiar in racing circles: Bugatti, Maserati, Bentley, Alfa Romeo, Duesenberg.

The instructions given here are for a car 7 inches long, which will require wheels about 1¾ inches in diameter. If you want a larger car, or if you happen to have some wheels which are larger, you can simply increase proportionately all the sizes as you see fit. Or you can make the car smaller, if that is your preference.

MATERIALS

One piece of 2 × 2-inch wood, 7 inches long, for the body
Material for the wheels, and 4 wood screws 1¼ inches long

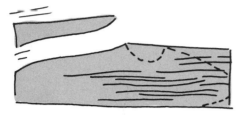

Use your coping saw to do as much of the preliminary shaping as possible.

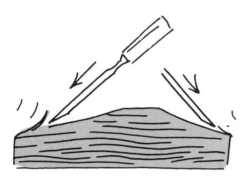

This is carving with the grain. It will produce neat, controlled chips.

This is carving into, or against, the grain. It will produce snags and splits.

1. Start by roughly shaping the body. You can speed things up by using your coping saw for some of the preliminary shaping. With the saw, you can narrow the rear end and taper the hood. But you'll need different tools to get the many rounded shapes which make these cars so elegant. Use your own judgment about these shapes. If you would rather have a more rounded rear end, or a hood of different proportions, by all means make it that way. This rough shaping can be done with a rasp or other shaping tool, or a hammer and chisel, or any tool you have that is capable of shaving off wood. (Watch the grain as you work. Cut *with* the grain, or across it, but not against it.) If you put your wood in a vise and use a sharp rasp, you should be able to shape the car body in half an hour, or 45 minutes at the most. If this is your first attempt at "carving" wood, do a little preliminary experimenting on some scrap wood. Try cutting in different directions—with the grain, against the grain—using whatever different tools you have available. In a little while you'll have an idea of just what works and what doesn't. Then you can begin to work in earnest on your car shape.

2. Now cut out the cockpit. A coping saw will work best for this. Then, if you want to add a windshield, use the same saw to cut a thin groove for it in front of the cockpit.

3. You can now proceed with the finishing shaping. Use a file or rough sandpaper and try to get the shapes as sleek and handsome as possible. Make sure that the right and left sides of the car are the same. Sand away any gouges or deep scratches left by your first, rough shaping operation. (Wrap your sandpaper around a block of wood and you will get a more even surface.)

4. Now make the wheels, as described in chapter 3. They should be about 1¾ inches in diameter.

5. The wheels for this car can best be attached with wood screws 1¼ inches long. Drill holes for the screws before you put them in place. This will enable you to screw them in easily without any danger of splitting the wood. (Be sure that the screw holes are all at the same distance up from the bottom of the car, to ensure that all four wheels rest on the ground at the same time.)

Mark the position of the screw holes with a pencil placed on a block of wood of the appropriate height.

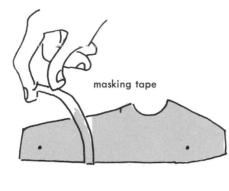

masking tape

A large, bold number will dress up your car considerably.

6. Now your car is all together, and you can check to see if the wheels turn freely and if all the shapes are just the way you want them. If everything seems all right, unscrew the wheels and do your final sanding and painting. Be patient and careful with your sanding now. Get all your shapes smooth and rounded, as graceful as you can manage. Start with rough sandpaper, then switch to medium, and finally to fine. Then paint, as described in chapter 2. If you want stripes, or the body in two or three colors, use masking tape so as to get straight edges.

7. If you are adding a windshield, make it now. It can be cut from any thin transparent plastic or acetate you can lay your hands on. Cut it to shape and glue it into the groove in front of the cockpit.

HOW TO MAKE A STEERING WHEEL

Any heavy wire that isn't too stiff can be used. Brass, copper, or galvanized iron wire will do.

Make a second sharp bend.

Bend one end of the remaining wire into a circle.

Snip off the excess.

First, make a sharp, right-angle bend. (A pair of long-nosed pliers will make the bending much simpler.)

This is how the wheel looks viewed from directly above.

The racing car shown above is similar to the one described on the previous pages. The big difference is that this one has fenders. The fenders used on this model were made from thin strips of plastic which were heated, bent to shape, allowed to cool, and cemented in place.

The car below is a more modern type. It shows just how sleek and shiny you can get a wooden model to look. About ten coats of metallic paint were sprayed on. The body is built of four pieces of wood assembled by the method shown on the next page.

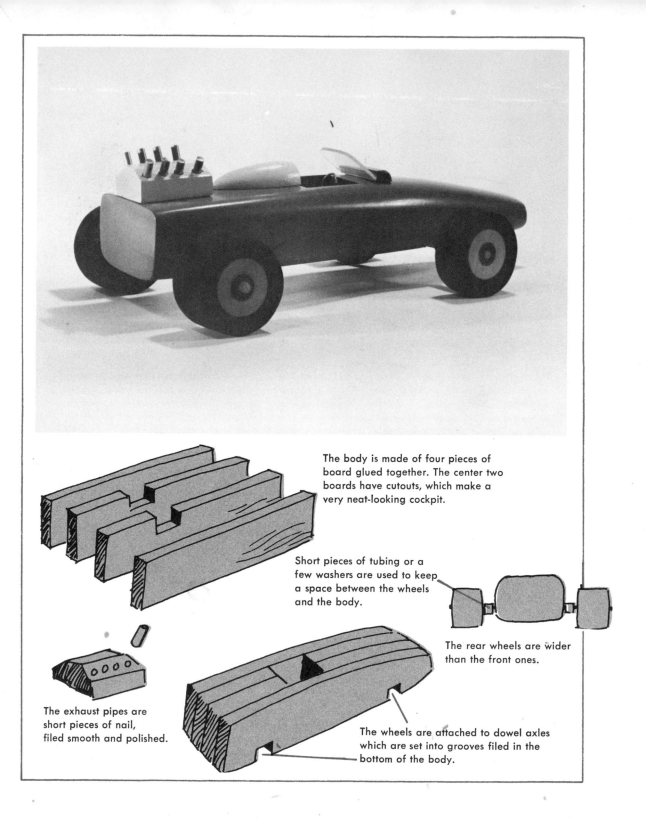

The body is made of four pieces of board glued together. The center two boards have cutouts, which make a very neat-looking cockpit.

Short pieces of tubing or a few washers are used to keep a space between the wheels and the body.

The rear wheels are wider than the front ones.

The exhaust pipes are short pieces of nail, filed smooth and polished.

The wheels are attached to dowel axles which are set into grooves filed in the bottom of the body.

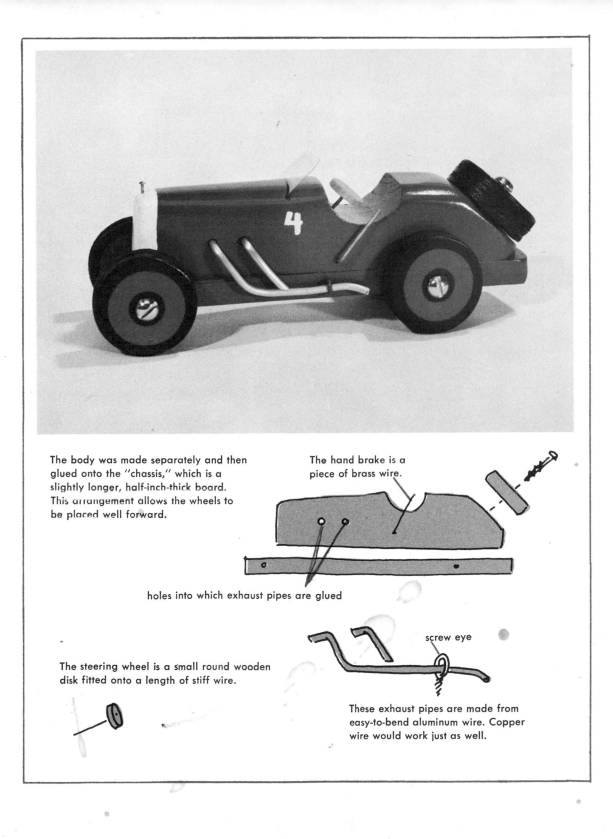

The body was made separately and then glued onto the "chassis," which is a slightly longer, half-inch-thick board. This arrangement allows the wheels to be placed well forward.

The hand brake is a piece of brass wire.

holes into which exhaust pipes are glued

The steering wheel is a small round wooden disk fitted onto a length of stiff wire.

screw eye

These exhaust pipes are made from easy-to-bend aluminum wire. Copper wire would work just as well.

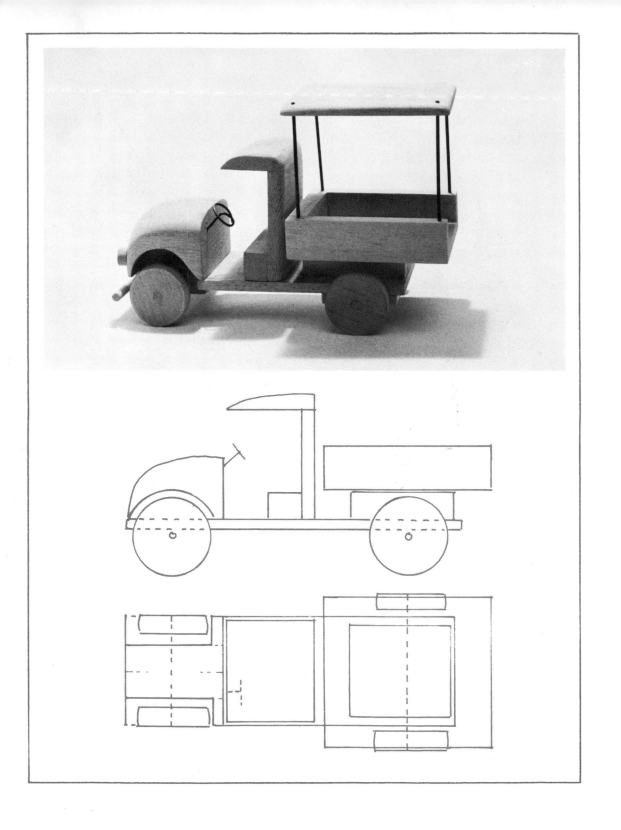

5. TRUCKS

The truck shown here has a simple open back, which makes it excellent for carting around all sorts of little odds and ends. However, it is an easy matter to modify the back section and produce a tow truck, a covered van, a small bus, a tank truck, or any of a variety of other special-purpose trucks.

The truck illustrated is fairly modern-looking. The hood is rounded and the front wheels fit under the bulky fenders. If you would prefer a different-looking, old-fashioned front end, you can refer to the next chapter and use some of the construction ideas shown there. As with all the projects in this book, it is possible to combine, rearrange, and modify different elements from different models.

MATERIALS

One piece of 1 × 2-inch pine, about a foot long, for the hood and the back of the cab

One 3-inch-wide board, about 2 feet long and quite thin, for a section of the cab, the chassis, and various other small parts ($\frac{1}{4}$- or $\frac{1}{8}$-inch thickness is best)

Materials for the wheels and axles

Scraps of wood and odds and ends

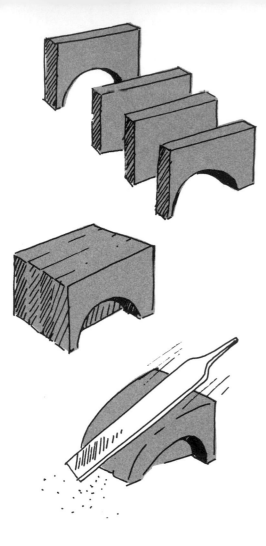

1. Start with the hood. This is made of four pieces cut from the 1×2-inch wood. Each piece should be about 2½ inches long. Cut a half circle in the two outside pieces. A coping saw will do this job easily.

2. Glue all four pieces together. Don't skimp on the glue, and apply clamps or weights for at least a half hour. A white glue such as Elmer's will work best.

3. When the glue is dry, use a rasp, a file, a sharp jackknife, a shaper, or whatever wood-shaping tools you have to get the shapes you want. Obtain the final rounded forms with sandpaper.

4. Make the chassis next. The chassis of a real car or truck is the steel framework to which the body and everything else is attached. For the models described in this book, we use the term to refer to the bottom strip of wood to which the wheels, hood, body, and cab are attached. In the case of this truck, the chassis is made out of a piece of thin wood about 7 inches long. Cut out two sections as shown to make room for the front wheels.

The front wheels go here. (The rear wheels are farther apart than the front ones.)

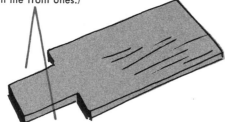

5. The cab is made from three small pieces of wood, glued and nailed firmly together. Make sure that the surfaces to be joined are first sanded perfectly flat. You won't get a strong joint if you try to glue together two rough or bumpy surfaces. When the glue has dried and you are sure the pieces are stuck firmly together, take a file or sandpaper and round off the front and back edges. (Don't attach either the cab or the hood to the chassis yet. You can do this after the final finishing and painting.)

6. Now make the wheels and axles. (See chapter 3 for directions.) The wheels should be about 1¾ inches in diameter. Use a ¼-inch dowel for the axles. (You can attach the wheels with screws if you prefer.)

7. Turn the chassis upside down and position the axles where you want them. Then glue down two strips of wood on either side of each axle. Don't place them so close to the axle that it can't turn freely.

8. Cut two small squares of wood and screw them down over the axles to the wooden strips. These will keep the wheels and axles in place.

If you don't want to mount the wheels this way, use one of the alternate methods shown on page 20, or attach the wheels with screws.

If the wood you are using isn't too thin, you can use two small nails for additional strength.

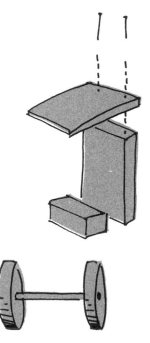

The front and rear wheels are attached in the same way.

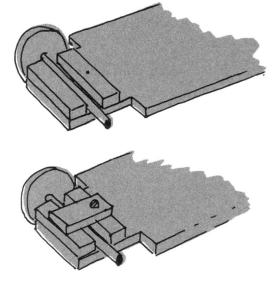

9. An open-backed pickup body can be formed as a simple box, using thin wood. Then attach a block of wood to the chassis and place the pickup body on top of it. This block serves to raise the body so that the rear wheels won't rub against it.

10. All that's left to do is to sand and paint. (See chapter 2 for information on finishing and painting.) The model will look best if you paint several parts a different color from the rest of the truck. Remember to do as much finishing and painting as possible before gluing all the parts together. Don't paint those surfaces which will be glued.

On the next few pages are some drawings of variations on this truck model. You might make one truck with several interchangeable bodies. If you attach the bodies with two small screws instead of glue, it is a simple matter to switch from one to another.

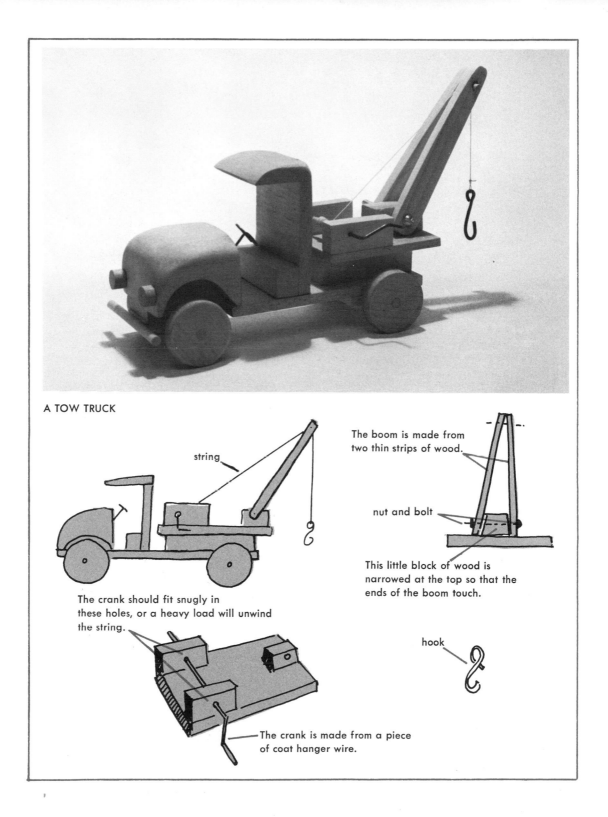

A TOW TRUCK

string

The boom is made from two thin strips of wood.

nut and bolt

This little block of wood is narrowed at the top so that the ends of the boom touch.

The crank should fit snugly in these holes, or a heavy load will unwind the string.

hook

The crank is made from a piece of coat hanger wire.

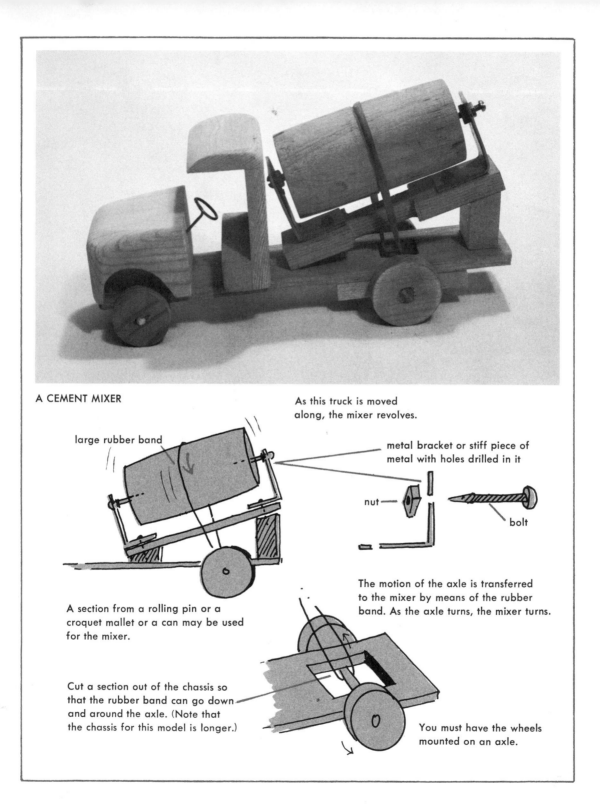

A CEMENT MIXER

As this truck is moved along, the mixer revolves.

large rubber band

metal bracket or stiff piece of metal with holes drilled in it

nut

bolt

A section from a rolling pin or a croquet mallet or a can may be used for the mixer.

The motion of the axle is transferred to the mixer by means of the rubber band. As the axle turns, the mixer turns.

Cut a section out of the chassis so that the rubber band can go down and around the axle. (Note that the chassis for this model is longer.)

You must have the wheels mounted on an axle.

PHIL'S MOVING Co.

Double wheels will give your truck a more realistic look.

If you can find a pair of small hinges, you can make rear doors that open and close.

A hinge or pivot arrangement such as this will turn your truck into a dump truck.

nut

bolt

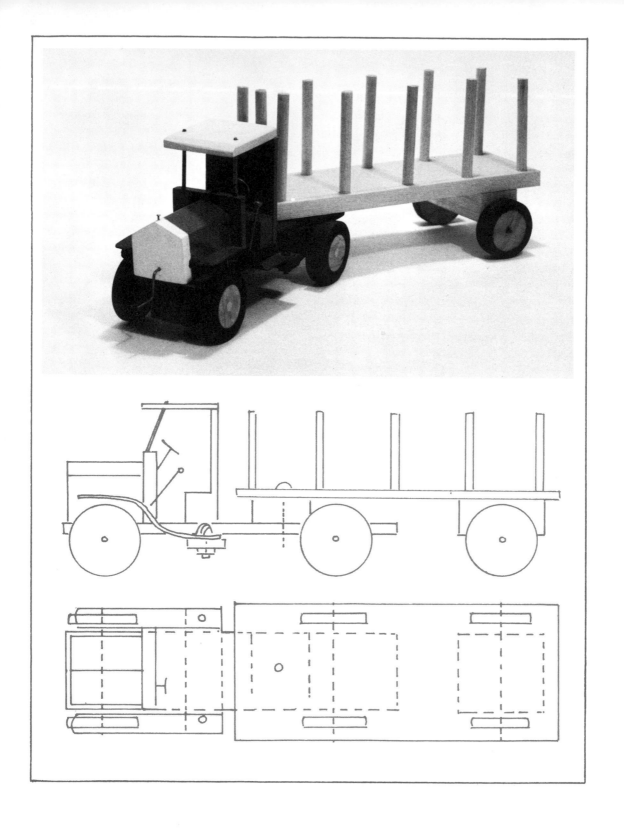

6. TRAILER TRUCKS

The trailer truck opposite is a pleasantly old-fashioned model with a simple rectangular trailer. The trailer doesn't have to be built as shown here, however. It can be modified to hold a few ladders. Then, with a coat of bright red paint, you will have a hook-and-ladder fire engine. A few of the other possibilities are shown at the end of this chapter.

The hood, fenders, and cab of this truck are a little more detailed than those of the model described in the previous chapter. But the construction isn't difficult. You simply have to take one step at a time. If you are careful and don't rush, you will end up with a handsome and rugged little trailer truck.

MATERIALS
One piece of 2-inch-wide, ¼- or ⅜-inch-thick wood, about
    3 feet long, for the cab, the chassis, and the trailer
Small block of wood for the hood (can be built up by
    gluing together two or more smaller pieces of wood)
Materials for the wheels and axles
Coat hanger wire
Old hacksaw blade or strip of tin
Miscellaneous hardware and scraps of wood

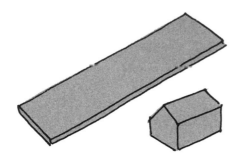

(The dimensions—where they are given—are only suggestions, and you should feel free to make changes as you see fit.)

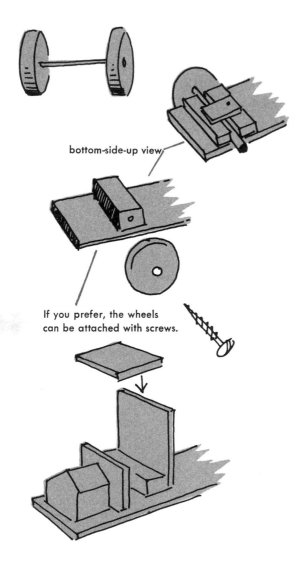

bottom-side-up view

If you prefer, the wheels can be attached with screws.

1. Cut out the chassis, which is simply an 8-inch-long piece of the thin 2-inch-wide wood.

2. Shape the hood as shown in the drawing. It looks a little like a house with a peaked roof.

3. The wheels and axles can be made next. (See chapter 3 for how to go about this.) The wheels should be about 1¾ inches in diameter. A ¼-inch dowel will make good axles.

4. To attach the wheels and axles to the chassis, first glue strips of wood on either side of each axle. Then screw square pieces of wood to the strips to hold everything in place. (If you prefer, you can attach the wheels by means of wood screws. If you use this method, you will have to glue blocks of wood instead of the axle-holding strips to the underneath side of the chassis. Then the screws can screw into the blocks.)

5. The cab is also made from the thin 2-inch-wide wood. Cut out a short piece of this and glue it to the back of the hood. Then cut out and assemble the seat, back, and roof of the cab. But don't glue this section to the chassis yet. Just prop it in place to see how it looks. You can attach it permanently after everything is sanded and painted.

6. Drill two holes in the roof of the cab. Then drill two holes in the top of the short piece of wood that you've glued to the back of the hood. Cut two short pieces of coat hanger wire and fit them into the holes you drilled.

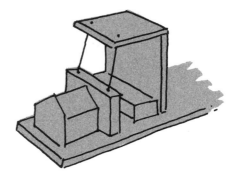

7. Next come the fenders and running boards. These require strong, thin strips of metal. A hacksaw blade is perfect—it is the right width and already has two holes drilled in it, one at either end. However, these blades are hardened, or "tempered," and it is necessary to soften the metal somewhat so that it can be bent and the teeth filed off. You can remove the "temper" by holding the blade over the kitchen stove with a pair of pliers until it gets red hot. Don't put it in water to cool—let it cool by itself in the air. Then break it in half. Put the pieces in a vise and file off the teeth, round the corners, bend as shown—and you have a very neat-looking combination fender and running board. Some high-quality hacksaw blades are made of a very hard alloy steel that will give you trouble in removing the stiffness. The kind of blade you want is the cheap, soft-steel blade on which only the cutting edge is tempered. If you can't find a suitable hacksaw blade, use metal from a tin can or any

41

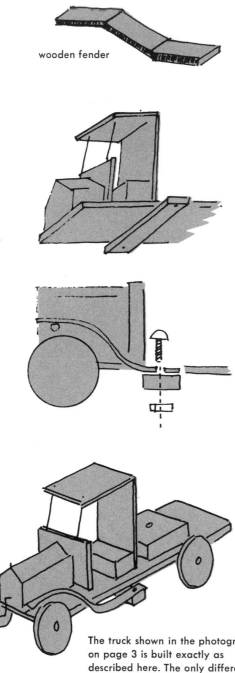

wooden fender

The truck shown in the photograph on page 3 is built exactly as described here. The only difference is that instead of a trailer it has on open-box back.

other thin metal you can lay your hands on. If worse comes to worst, you can make a perfectly fine fender and running board out of three pieces of wood, as shown in the drawing.

8. Glue a strip of wood underneath the chassis. Drill a hole at each end of it and attach each running board and fender to it with a small nut and bolt. (A nut and bolt are needed here because a wood screw would split the wood.) If you can't find a suitable nut and bolt, you can saw a groove in each end of the wood and then glue the metal into this. The front end of the fender is supported by a small piece of dowel set into the hood, or else by a small block of wood glued in place.

9. Glue a small block of wood to the rear of the chassis. This is to support the front end of the trailer and to elevate it above the rear wheels of the truck. Drill a hole in the center of the block. This is where the trailer will be attached by means of a nut and bolt.

10. The trailer is quite simple to put together. It is made from the same thin wood that was used for the truck chassis. The drawings opposite show how a plain open trailer is made.

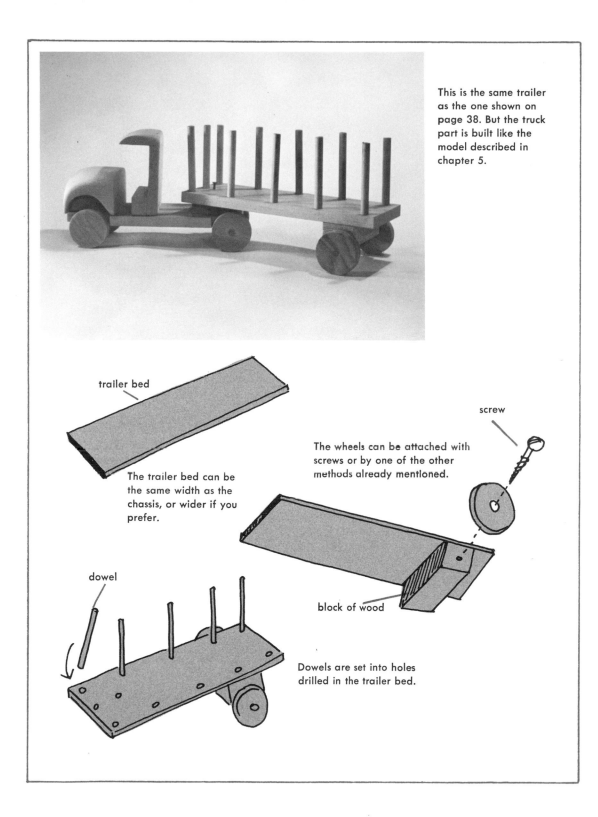

This is the same trailer as the one shown on page 38. But the truck part is built like the model described in chapter 5.

trailer bed

The trailer bed can be the same width as the chassis, or wider if you prefer.

screw

The wheels can be attached with screws or by one of the other methods already mentioned.

block of wood

dowel

Dowels are set into holes drilled in the trailer bed.

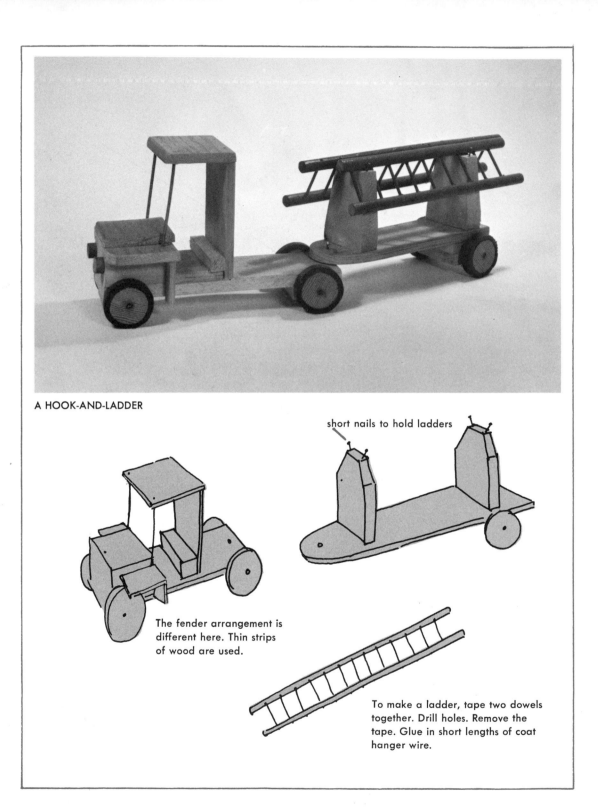

A HOOK-AND-LADDER

short nails to hold ladders

The fender arrangement is different here. Thin strips of wood are used.

To make a ladder, tape two dowels together. Drill holes. Remove the tape. Glue in short lengths of coat hanger wire.

There are many possible variations for the trailer. A ladder that can be cranked up is quite easy to put together. The crank arrangement and the pivot are the same as are used for the tow truck shown on page 35.

string

crank arrangement to raise missile

A heavy load requires double wheels.

A tin can may be used to make a tank truck. The kind of can that tennis balls come in is ideal, or you can use a section of a cardboard tube.

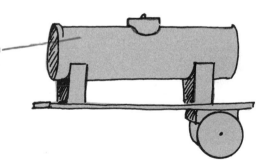

Some trailers are very long.

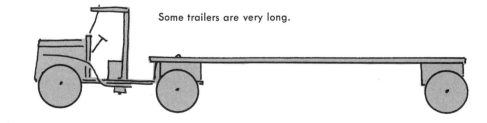

A "TIN LIZZIE"

The hood is a block of wood.

The body is a simple box with the back end rounded off.

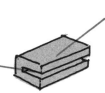

chassis

Although this model is of a car and not a truck, it is described here because it uses many of the construction methods explained in the two previous chapters. This car was the first mass-produced vehicle in America. It was built by Henry Ford and given the nickname "Tin Lizzie." The model shown here isn't a very exact copy of this car, but it has the tall, large-wheeled, open look of the cars of the period. Henry Ford said his customers could order his car in any color they wanted as long as it was black. But this model is painted a bright yellow, and the leather top is a warm brown. The fenders are black.

A small block of wood with a groove sawed into it is glued to each side of the chassis. The fender is cemented into this groove.

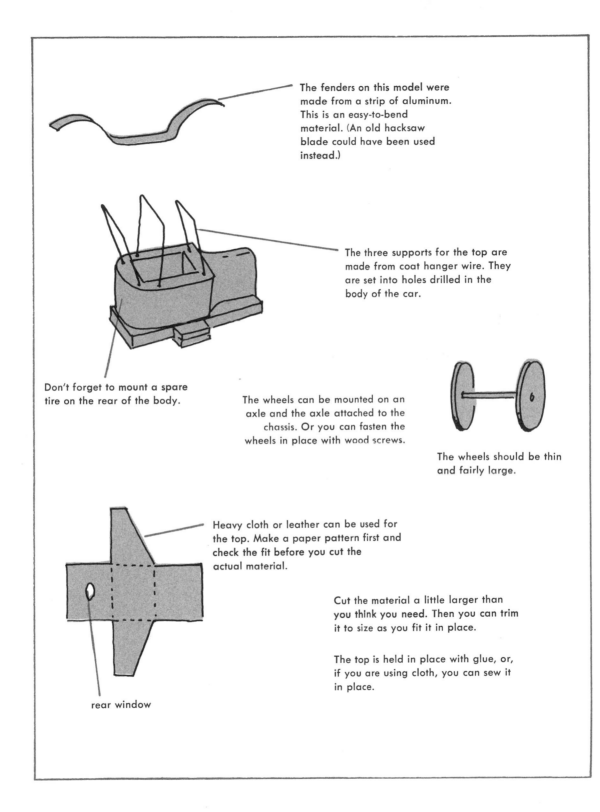

The fenders on this model were made from a strip of aluminum. This is an easy-to-bend material. (An old hacksaw blade could have been used instead.)

The three supports for the top are made from coat hanger wire. They are set into holes drilled in the body of the car.

Don't forget to mount a spare tire on the rear of the body.

The wheels can be mounted on an axle and the axle attached to the chassis. Or you can fasten the wheels in place with wood screws.

The wheels should be thin and fairly large.

Heavy cloth or leather can be used for the top. Make a paper pattern first and check the fit before you cut the actual material.

Cut the material a little larger than you think you need. Then you can trim it to size as you fit it in place.

The top is held in place with glue, or, if you are using cloth, you can sew it in place.

rear window

7. TRACTORS

Tractors come in many different sizes and shapes. Some of them are used to pull farm equipment, and some have various attachments and modifications so that they can be used for all sorts of special jobs, such as ditch digging, earth moving, or loading.

The tractor shown here is a simple, straightforward type. It is designed so that the front wheels can be turned. The "exhaust pipe" is attached to the front wheels—when it is turned, the wheels turn.

This tractor is in many ways quite similar to a bulldozer. If you made a different set of wheels and added a a front scoop, you would have a very serious-looking piece of earth-moving equipment.

MATERIALS

One piece of ½ × 2-inch wood, about a foot long, for the chassis and other small parts

One piece of 2 × 3-inch wood, about 3½ inches long, for the hood

Materials for wheels and axles

6-inch-long piece of ⅜-inch dowel for the steering shaft

Miscellaneous hardware and scraps of wood

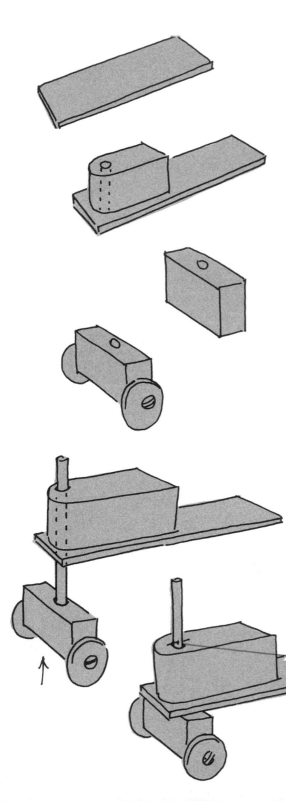

1. Make the chassis first. This is simply a 7-inch-long piece of the ½ × 2-inch wood. (We call it the chassis because most of the other parts of the tractor are attached to it.)

2. Make the hood next. It is shaped as shown in the drawing—rounded in front and on top. Glue it to the chassis. Drill a ⅜-inch hole through both the hood and chassis.

3. Cut a block of the 2 × 3-inch wood as shown. This is to hold the front wheels. Drill a ⅜-inch-diameter hole about ½ inch deep in the top of this block.

4. Make the front wheels next. (Chapter 3 has all the information about how to do this.) The wheels can now be attached to the block of wood with two wood screws.

5. Now glue the 6-inch-long piece of ⅜-inch dowel into the hole in the top of the wooden block. The dowel piece can now be pushed through the holes that were drilled through the hood and chassis. If the fit is tight, sand down the dowel. The tractor is steered by turning this dowel.

Drill a small hole at the point where the dowel comes up out of the hood. Then fit a wooden peg or piece of wire in this hole to keep the dowel as well as the front wheels from slipping down when the tractor is picked up.

6. Make the rear wheels next. They may be cut out of a board that is at least 3½ inches wide. They can be attached by means of a dowel axle, or simply by wood screws.

7. Make the seat from a small block of wood. Glue a piece of thin wood to the back of it to make a backrest.

8. The little canopy—which is an optional piece of equipment—is made from a piece of thin wood. It is held in place with four thin nails or brads, or else with coat hanger wire. If you use nails, cut off the heads. Don't try to hammer the nails or the pieces of wire into place— the wood would probably split. Drill holes for them and use glue.

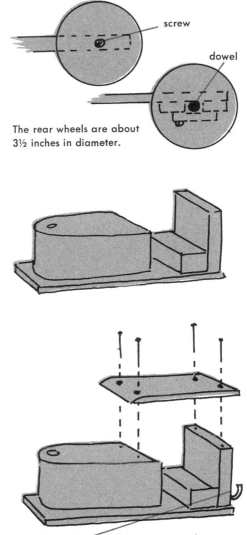

The rear wheels are about 3½ inches in diameter.

Attach a screw hook to the rear of the tractor so that it can pull a wagon or harrow or other farm machinery.

screw hook

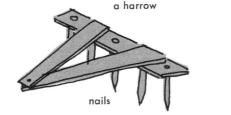

a harrow

nails

a scoop for the front of the tractor

The two side arms are screwed to the chassis.

This wagon can be towed behind the tractor or the bulldozer.

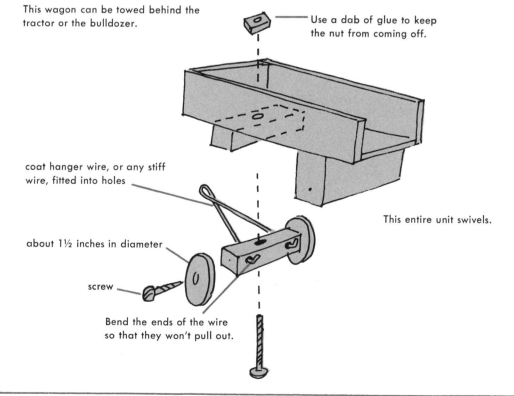

Use a dab of glue to keep the nut from coming off.

This entire unit swivels.

coat hanger wire, or any stiff wire, fitted into holes

about 1½ inches in diameter

screw

Bend the ends of the wire so that they won't pull out.

A BULLDOZER

The scoop on this bulldozer moves up and down.
A string runs from the bottom edge of the scoop,
up over a little guide, and onto the shaft of the
steering wheel. Turn the wheel one way and the
scoop goes up. Turn it the other way and it goes
down.

Drill a hole for the steering wheel shaft.

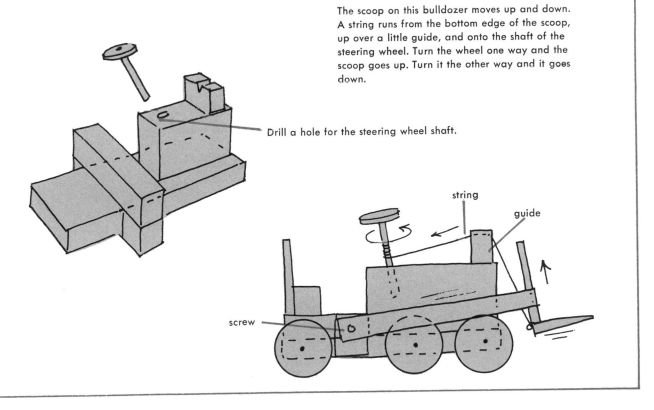

string

guide

screw

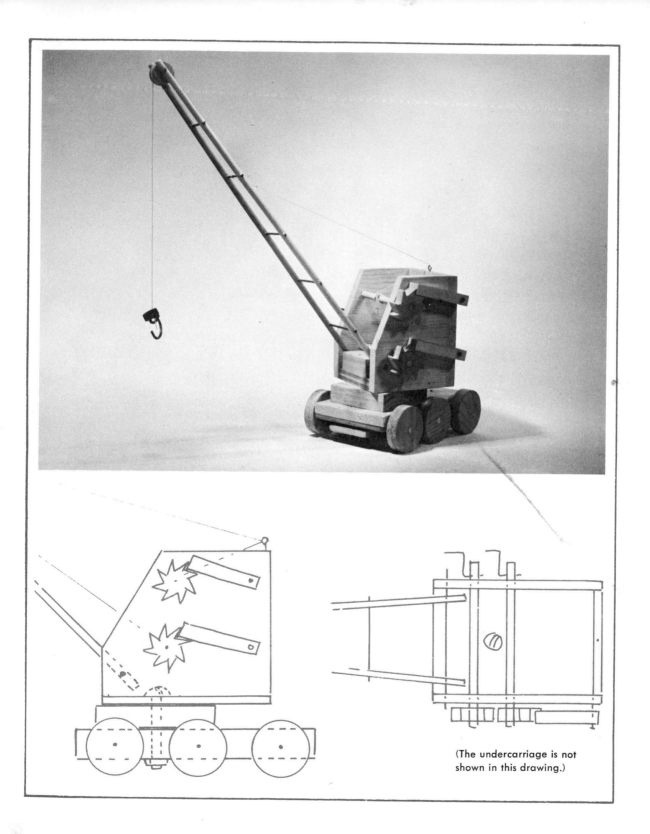

(The undercarriage is not shown in this drawing.)

8. DERRICKS

This derrick has all the action and motion of the real thing. The boom can be raised and lowered. The hook can be cranked up and down. The body can be swung in any direction, and it can be rolled along on its six sturdy wheels.

The model shown here is unpainted and looks perfectly fine this way. But there is no reason why you couldn't paint it if you wanted to. You could also mount this derrick on the back of a truck. Truck bodies like the ones shown in chapters 5 and 6 would be fine, though they would have to be made a little larger than specified.

There are quite a few parts to this model, but none of them is difficult to make. Don't be intimidated by what may look like a complicated project. Worry about only one part at a time, and before you know it everything will fit into place and you will have your finished derrick.

MATERIALS
One piece of ½ × 4-inch pine, about 2 feet long, for the
    body and chassis
Two ¼-inch dowels for the boom and crankshafts
Coat hanger wire
String
Miscellaneous hardware and scraps of wood
Material for the wheels and axles
One bolt 2½ inches long with nut and washers

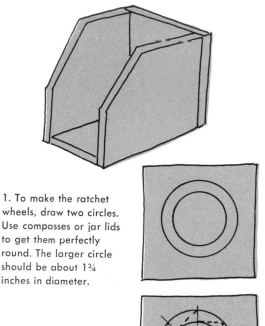

1. Start by making the body of the derrick. This is really no more than a three-sided box. It is built of pieces of the ½ × 4-inch pine, glued and nailed together.

2. The next things to make are the two crank mechanisms. The wheels that look like gears are called "ratchet wheels." Their purpose is to keep the boom and hook from unwinding when the derrick is carrying a heavy load. They are cut out of the ½-inch-thick wood. Ratchet wheels let you crank in one direction only. The eight teeth are angled in such a way that the thin piece of wood, called a "pawl," prevents the ratchet wheel from turning to the right. When you do want the wheel to turn to the right, you must first raise the pawl. The ratchet wheels, which are about 1¾ inches in diameter, are made as shown here.

1. To make the ratchet wheels, draw two circles. Use compasses or jar lids to get them perfectly round. The larger circle should be about 1¾ inches in diameter.

2. Divide the circles into eight equal parts. Then draw lines between the inner and outer circles as shown by the dotted lines.

3. Saw along the lines shown in color.

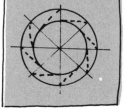

This is the pawl. Be sure it is free to move up and down.

nail or screw

The ratchet wheel can turn freely to the left. The slanted side of the gear tooth will push the pawl up out of the way as the wheel turns. There is a clickity-clack sound as it turns.

However, the wheel can't turn to the right unless you lift up the pawl. The vertical edge of the ratchet tooth is pushing directly against the pawl, preventing motion to the right.

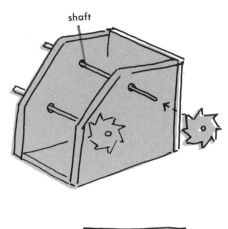

3. The shaft to wind up the hook, and the one to raise or lower the boom are each made from a 5-inch length of ¼-inch dowel. Drill holes in the derrick body for these shafts. The holes should be slightly larger than the dowels so that the dowels can turn freely. Glue the ratchet wheels to the ends of the shafts.

4. The pawls are made from pieces of wood approximately ½ × ½ × 2½ inches. Drill a hole through one end and then nail or screw each pawl in place. The hole for the nail or screw must be large enough so that the pawl can move freely up and down as the ratchet wheel turns.

Here's a close-up view of the ratchet wheels and the pawls.

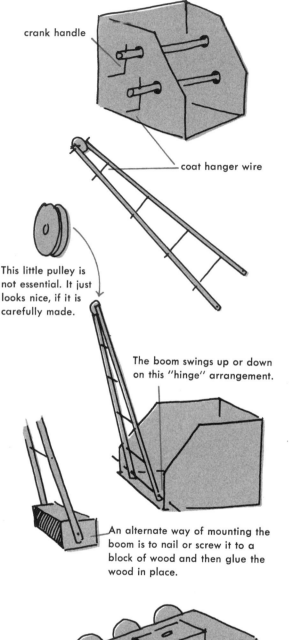

crank handle

coat hanger wire

This little pulley is not essential. It just looks nice, if it is carefully made.

The boom swings up or down on this "hinge" arrangement.

An alternate way of mounting the boom is to nail or screw it to a block of wood and then glue the wood in place.

5. The crank handles can be made from short pieces of coat hanger wire. Drill holes for them in the ends of the shafts. Put the shafts in place again on the derrick, then glue the handles in permanently.

6. The boom is made from two ¼-inch dowels, each about 15 inches long. Tape the two dowels together, then drill holes at intervals through both pieces. A ³⁄₃₂-inch bit will be the right size. (If you don't have the right size of bit, use a small nail with the head cut off.) Remove the tape. To make the cross braces, cut some coat hanger wire to the proper lengths and glue the pieces into the holes you've drilled. The pulley at the top of the boom can be made by cutting out a small wheel and then filing a groove in it.

7. The boom is attached to the body of the derrick by means of a piece of coat hanger wire. Drill two holes in the front of the derrick body. The wire goes through these as well as through the two bottom holes in the boom.

8. Next make the chassis of the derrick, which is a piece of ½ × 4-inch pine about 7 inches long. The best way to attach the wheels is with screws, but if you prefer, you can use dowel axles. The body of the derrick sits on a block of wood glued to the top of the chassis.

9. The derrick body is attached to the chassis by means of a 2½-inch bolt. Drill a hole through the bottom of the derrick body, the block, and right through the chassis. Insert the bolt through it. Don't tighten the nut so much that the body won't be able to swivel. You can make sure the nut won't work loose and drop off by putting a dab of glue on the end of the bolt. Use washers under the head of the bolt and under the nut.

10. Any thin but strong string can be used to raise and lower the hook and to control the boom. If you can get some of the braided nylon squidding line that fishermen use, you will have the ideal thing. The hook can be made from coat hanger wire. It won't be heavy enough by itself to drop down when the crank is unwound, so you will have to place a heavy nut or a few washers on the string above the hook.

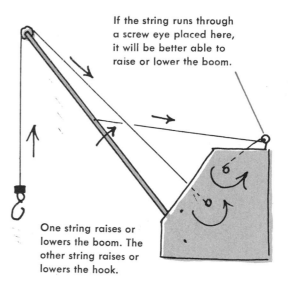

If the string runs through a screw eye placed here, it will be better able to raise or lower the boom.

One string raises or lowers the boom. The other string raises or lowers the hook.

weight

The hook can be made from any stiff wire.

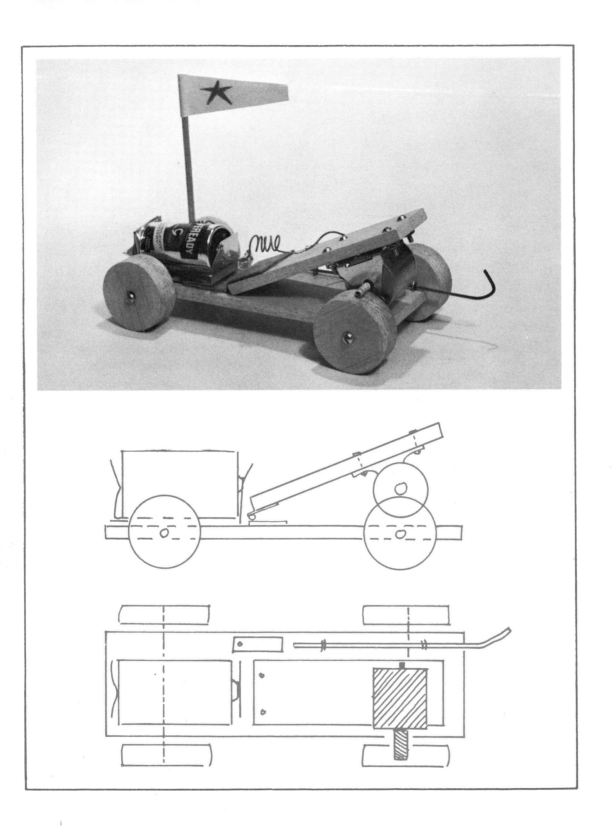

9. A MOTOR-DRIVEN MODEL

This little vehicle has a small battery-powered motor which will drive it at a very respectable speed. The rod which sticks out at the rear of this model is the off-on switch. Pull it back, and the battery is disconnected and the motor stops.

A motor like the one used here is available in most hobby shops for about a dollar. Get one that will work on 1½ to 3 volts. A single flashlight battery, which is 1½ volts, may not provide adequate power. Two batteries will give you a little extra speed and power.

If you can't get a motor like this, you may be able to find an old motor in a broken or discarded toy. Many battery-driven toys have small motors you can use. Even if the toy is a battered old wreck you may be able to salvage a perfectly good, workable motor. But be sure it will work with one or two batteries. There is nothing wrong with motors that use more batteries—the problem comes in finding room for them. You'd have to build a fairly large model if you wanted to fit in four batteries.

If your model works with power and efficiency, you might decide you want to add a lightweight body, which can be slipped over the chassis. Very thin wood or cardboard is best for bodies of this sort.

MATERIALS

One piece of ¼ × 4-inch wood, about 9 inches long, for the chassis

Piece of 1-inch-thick board out of which the wheels can be cut

Small battery-powered motor, batteries, and electric hook-up wire

Small hinge or scrap of leather

Coat hanger wire

Miscellaneous hardware, scraps of wood and metal, and a few odds and ends

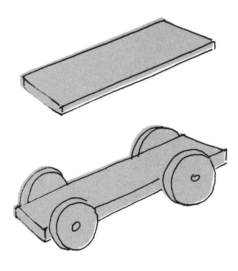

The motor is mounted on the underneath side of this piece of wood.

motor   nails or screws

1. Cut out the chassis from the ¼ × 4-inch wood. Shape it as shown.

2. Make the wheels out of the 1-inch-thick board. They should be about 2 inches in diameter. Attach them to the chassis with wood screws. Because the chassis is made of thin wood, it is important that you drill a small hole for each screw before screwing it in. Otherwise there is a good chance the wood will split.

3. Cut a piece of thin wood about 5 inches long and 1½ inches wide. Nail or screw your motor to one end of this as shown, in such a way that the drive shaft projects beyond the side of the wood.

4. Fasten a small hinge to the other end of the wood. Be sure it is a very loose-acting one—a tight hinge won't work. If you don't have this kind of hinge, a piece of leather will do just as well. In fact, you can even use a piece of heavy fabric such as canvas or linen. If you use leather or fabric, glue it securely to the chassis and to the board holding the motor, as shown. This arrangement allows the drive shaft of the motor to rest on the car wheel. The weight of the wood and motor causes the shaft to make a firm contact with the wheel.

5. The motor drive shaft will be too small and smooth to turn the car wheel without slipping, so you must increase the friction between the two somehow. The simplest way is to wrap the shaft with masking or adhesive tape. Another way is to find a short piece of rubber or plastic tubing which can be glued around the shaft.

6. In order to attach the wires to the batteries you need battery holders. They can be made as shown below, from small strips of metal. Copper, aluminum, or the metal from a tin can will work fine.

hinge

motor

piece of leather used as a hinge

tape wrapped around motor shaft

This is how the holder looks with the battery in place.

Put a rubber band around the battery and holder to make sure the holder fits tightly around the battery.

Punch holes in toward where the battery will be so that the jagged edges of the holes will make firm contact with the battery terminals.

Punch two additional holes so that you can connect the wires.

Insulate this part of the holder by wrapping it with tape.

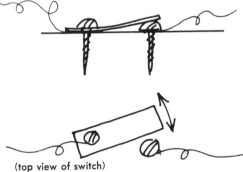

screw

hook-up wire wrapped around coat hanger wire

strip of tin

two staples or bent-over nails to hold coat hanger wire in place

A more simple switch that will work just as well can be made with two screws and a short piece of tin. The tin can be swung back and forth to make or break contact.

(top view of switch)

7. The switch is made from a scrap of metal of the kind used for the battery holders, and a 6-inch length of coat hanger wire. The batteries, motor, and switch are connected to one another as shown in the drawing below. When the coat hanger wire is pushed in, it touches the small strip of metal and completes the circuit. The current flows through the motor, and the model starts on its way. Before you put the coat hanger wire in place, be sure to sandpaper it carefully to remove any paint or varnish—which would act as an insulating layer and prevent the current from flowing.

Be sure that insulation or paint is scraped off any parts that are to make electrical contact.

How to connect battery, motor, and switch:

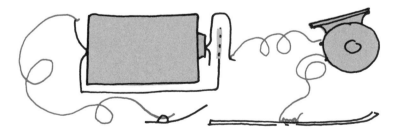

The switch can be placed anywhere on the chassis that is convenient.

8. The drawings below show a few of the different kinds of bodies that can be made to fit over the motorized chassis. They are basic boxlike shapes that can be easily lifted off in one piece if you need to make any adjustments of the switch, batteries, or motor. The body should be as lightweight as possible. If you don't want to bother with a separate body, you can just stick a little flag on the chassis and call it a moon buggy!

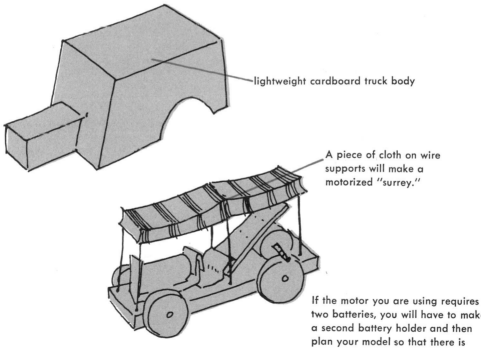

lightweight cardboard truck body

A piece of cloth on wire supports will make a motorized "surrey."

If the motor you are using requires two batteries, you will have to make a second battery holder and then plan your model so that there is a place to put it.

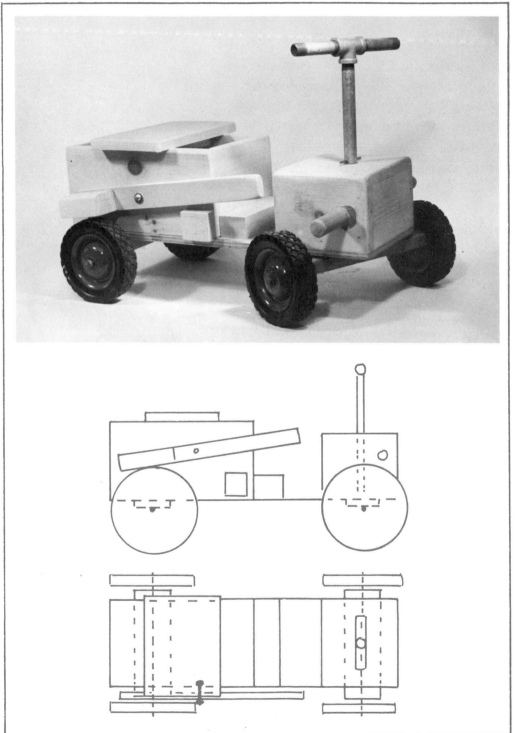

10. A LARGE MODEL
TO RIDE ON

The model shown here is about three times as large as most of the others described thus far. But even so it is about as small a model as anyone can comfortably ride on. It is fun to build, and if you have a hill where you can use it you will be able to move along at a fine clip.

Because this model is so large and will have to support your weight, the materials used must be fairly rugged. There is no point in trying to make this car out of thin, warped wood and small, rusty nails—you would end up with a pile of kindling after going over the first big bump.

The wheels, axles, and steering gear are the most important parts of this model. The sort of wheels shown in the photograph can be bought in most hardware stores. They are very strong and work quite well. The smallest size, about 6 inches in diameter, costs a little less than two dollars apiece. Larger sizes are also available. This type of wheel has a hole which allows it to fit on a ½-inch-diameter steel rod. The rod, from which two axles can be cut, will cost a little more than a dollar.

Another kind of wheel and axle, which will work just as well and will cost a good deal less, is the kind you can find on old baby carriages or strollers. You should be able to get an old "vehicle" of this sort from a thrift shop, junkyard, or garbage dump.

Steering is controlled by a series of pipe fittings. Five separate fittings are needed. They all screw into one another to make a strong and quite dependable arrangement. These fittings can be bought in any well-equipped hardware or plumbing supply store. They should cost something like three dollars altogether.

The plans show just how the truck in the photograph was assembled. But, as with all the models in this book, there is no reason to stick to them exactly in every detail. You might, for example, find a set of wheels different from the ones described, and then you would be forced to make changes. Or you might decide you want a larger—or smaller—model. Or perhaps you want to change the body to make a racing car, or a Rolls-Royce, or a moon buggy. The only part of this model that you might find hard to modify is the steering arrangement. This must be quite strong because the front wheels and steering wheel take a good deal of punishment.

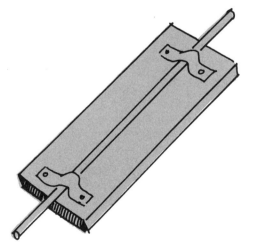

1. Cut out the wooden piece to which the front axle will be attached. The axle is fastened to the underneath side of this by two straps of metal. In any hardware store you can get what are called "reinforcing straps." They should measure about ¾ inch wide and 4 inches long, and have several holes in them. You will have to put them in a vise and bend them so that they will fit around the axle and hold it securely to the piece of wood.

2. Put the wheels on the axle and see how long it should be. Then cut the axle to the correct length, allowing it to project about ¼ inch beyond each wheel. Drill a hole at a point about ⅛ inch in from each end of the axle. Put a cotter pin or piece of wire through each hole to keep the wheels from coming off.

3. The five pipe fittings you need for the steering are shown below. The flange is securely screwed to the top of the front wheel assembly.

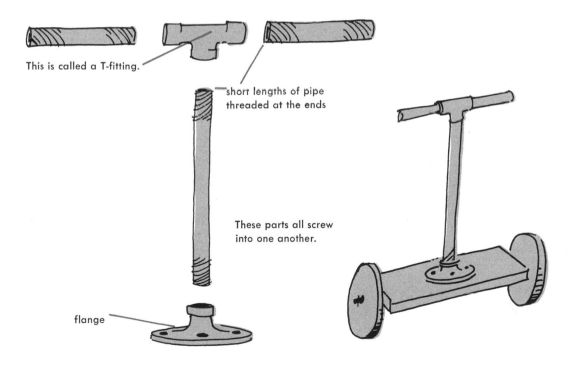

This is called a T-fitting.

short lengths of pipe threaded at the ends

These parts all screw into one another.

flange

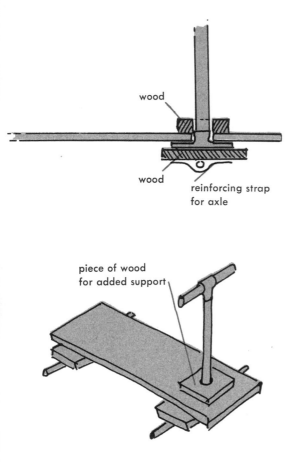

wood

wood

reinforcing strap
for axle

piece of wood
for added support

4. Cut the wood for the chassis next. Drill a hole in it through which the steering pipe will fit. This must be done very carefully. If the hole is ragged or too big, the pipe will wobble and won't stay firmly upright. You may find that you need a second piece of wood to give the pipe a little extra support.

5. Cut out another piece of wood and attach the rear axle and wheels to it in the same way as the front ones. Then glue and screw the wood to the underside of the chassis.

6. All that's left to do now is to make the body. The drawings show how this is done.

If you look closely at the photograph on page 66, you will see that there is a nail which goes through the steering shaft at a point just above the hood. This nail (with the head cut off) is set into a hole drilled in the shaft. Its purpose is to keep the shaft from slipping down when the coaster is picked up or raised off the ground. The nail is bent slightly so that it will stay in place.

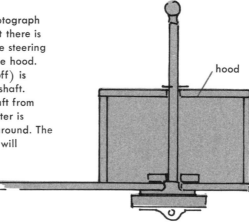

hood

This is the seat. The piece of wood on the bottom is to keep it from sliding off to the side.

brake

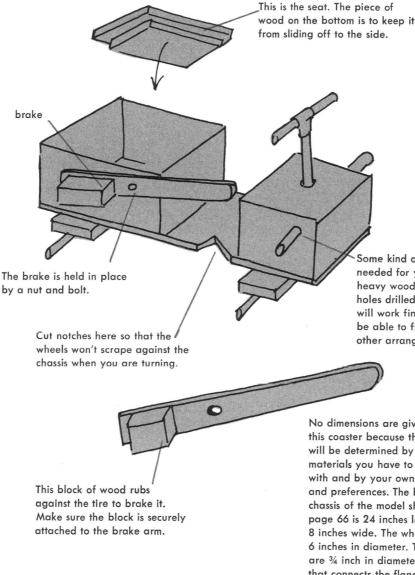

The brake is held in place by a nut and bolt.

Cut notches here so that the wheels won't scrape against the chassis when you are turning.

Some kind of support is needed for your feet. A heavy wooden rod set into holes drilled in the hood will work fine, or you may be able to figure out some other arrangement.

This block of wood rubs against the tire to brake it. Make sure the block is securely attached to the brake arm.

No dimensions are given for this coaster because the size will be determined by the materials you have to work with and by your own ideas and preferences. The basic chassis of the model shown on page 66 is 24 inches long and 8 inches wide. The wheels are 6 inches in diameter. The pipes are ¾ inch in diameter. The pipe that connects the flange to the T-fitting is 12 inches long.

The models on these pages are rather fanciful —not very serious. The car above and the one below are really exaggerations of a high-performance racer and a dragster. No attempt has been made to get a very accurate copy of an existing car. A general impression and feeling rather than realism was the main concern.

The "vehicle" above is a battering ram such as some demented inventor in the sixteenth century might have designed. (It could be an artillery piece if a cannon barrel had been used instead of the wooden ram.) The wheels of this model are attached to two pieces of wood which are hinged to the chassis. These two pieces of wood are connected with string to a horizontal shaft which can be rotated. As this shaft is turned, the string is either drawn in or let out, causing the wheels to draw together or spread apart. This raises or lowers the ram. The short vertical dowel underneath the chassis, through which the string runs, lets the string pull at an efficient angle. The little square roof is an unnecessary addition, but might serve to shade the operator from the sun or protect against enemy missiles.

This is a model of a vehicle that is supposed to fly, float, or roll along on dry land. It has a propeller in front for flying, and another smaller, three-bladed propeller at the rear for use in water. There is a rugged, three-wheel undercarriage with mudguards. The smokestack and boiler you can see sticking out of the boat hull are for the steam engine, which provides the power.